HOMER

PAMELA COLERICK

ISBN 978-1-63961-314-4 (paperback)
ISBN 978-1-63961-315-1 (digital)

Christian Faith Publishing
832 Park Avenue
Meadville, PA 16335
www.christianfaithpublishing.com

Printed in the United States of America

    I'm writing this book series in memory of my son-in-law, Steve. He passed away in June 2020 at the age of thirty-eight, leaving behind his beautiful young family and many friends and extended family. My husband and I loved him very much. We took in his dog, Homer, in July 2019. It was a difficult decision for Steve to let go of Homer, but he was happy to know that he was going to a good home and staying in the family. He planned to visit often, but unfortunately, his life was cut short, and he last saw Homer in December 2019 for Christmas. Steve always talked of creating a book series about Homer because Homer is such a funny dog with a big personality. They went on so many adventures together. There are so many stories to share. Homer has made new memories and has gone on even more adventures since living with my husband and me. I'd like to bring many of those adventures (old and new) to life through this book series, as it has been a recent interest of mine to create children's books.

Hello, my name is Homer, and I am a mix between a pit bull and an American bulldog. I think my owner, Steve, looked me up on Ancestors.com. We look so much alike! He adopted me from a shelter in Southern California about eleven years ago. Wow, time sure flies. I remember how happy I was when I first went home with Steve and met his girlfriend, Kelly. I think she was fascinated with me from the start.

3

I'm quite good-looking with charcoal-gray and white markings. It was commonplace for people to say to Steve and Kelly on our walks, "What a good-looking dog!" I was pretty used to that.

Grrrrr!!

It was obvious to me that Steve would try to work out to look like me. He'd go to the gym as often as he could to lift weights. My muscles came pretty easy for me; walking seemed to keep me buff. Must be my breed. By the way, anytime you see a dog like me, or any dog, don't just go up to them and pet them. Most dogs like it, but I really don't unless I know you well. I tend to give a warning growl to let people know that.

Speaking of walking, I'm pretty sure Steve was very impressed with how many bags he would go through on our strolls in our neighborhood. We'd stop once, and I'd find just the right place to leave my poo. Next thing you know, I did it again. By the third time, it might be small, but I knew how much Steve liked to use up all the bags he brought, so I didn't hold back.

In California, my first home, Steve would take me most days to work with him in his white pickup truck. I loved sitting in the front seat with him and looking out the window, snot dripping from my sniffer, drool hanging out the sides of my mouth, and the wind blowing my ears up. Those were good days!

I've met many dogs during my lifetime, living with Steve. One of my first friends was Nixon, a mixed breed of I'm not sure what. He was reddish-brown, and his ears hung down next to his face. I always tried to get him to wrestle, play, jump, you know, just dog stuff. But Nixon always refused. He was kinda uptight and timid, I guess. We lived together for about a year, then he moved out with his owner, and another dog named Leroy, a Chihuahua. Leroy and I were buddies too.

Another buddy I had was Stuart, a Welsh terrier, I think. He was a little frightened of me because of my size, but I wasn't a bully. I guess if you're a tiny breed, you might be a little jealous of me and my muscles. He was snooty and tried to stare me down a lot. For a dog I could have eaten in one bite, he sure was confident.

I have had so many friends along the way during my life with Steve. There was one dog named Kiarra who looked like a girl version of me, and we had the best time! She would visit often, and she could jump as high as me, eat as much as me, run as fast as me, and wrestle a little better than me. She was tough.

Steve ended up marrying that pretty girl Kelly, the one who was head over heels in love with me the day she met me. They eventually had two daughters together, Lilly and Ayla. They sure are dandy little girls, and I would give them sloppy kisses when they weren't paying attention.

19

Eventually, Steve and Kelly needed to move into a bigger home, and unfortunately, a lot of places don't want dogs like me. That's the problem with being as good-looking and muscular as me; I get people nervous. Plus I didn't like being cramped in small places, and I started to get a little grumpy. Having two little girls now, Steve had to make the tough decision of finding me a new home. That's okay, though. I found another place to live.

21

My new home is in the country in Western New York. Now every day I look up in the sky and all around my big backyard where I spend most of my time with new dog friends, Shelby and Abbey. They also have three cats that I put up with. After all, they were there first, and they all accepted me. Oh, did I mention that my new owner is the dad of the girl whom Steve married, who was so topsy-turvy in love with me? That's right! I'm still in the family and very happy.

Now instead of going for rides with Steve, I go for rides with my new buddy, Don. Most of the time, I'm in the front seat, looking out the window, snot dripping from my sniffer, drool hanging out the sides of my mouth, and the wind blowing my ears up. These are great days!

ABOUT THE AUTHOR

Pam Colerick is a wife, mother, and grandmother first. She has been an RN for twenty-eight years, working first in a hospital, then in an oncology unit for eleven years, and for over ten years where she is now, as an infusion nurse at a rheumatology office.

She has always loved animals, so it's no surprise that she would be writing about a dog. What is unpredictable is that she would be writing about Homer. See, initially, she wasn't all that fond of Homer. In all probability, they wouldn't have him if it wasn't for her husband, Don. He instantaneously liked Homer; Pam, let's just say he has grown on her.

When she was in high school, she perpetually wrote down her feelings, either in poems or just journaling or blogging, in today's terms. She always thought that she would write something worthwhile someday. That day is now. This children's book is for her son-in-law, Steve, whom they miss every day, and for her five grandchildren: Ayden, Tommie, Asher, Lilly, and Ayla.

CPSIA information can be obtained
at www.ICGtesting.com
Printed in the USA
BVHW020628160522
637021BV00001B/7